A.J. Paquette

A.J. Paquette

MARKINGS

Scenes and Recollections of Winnipeg's North End

Published by Loch & Mayberry Fine Art Inc.

I would like to dedicate this book to all those characters who are,
in a sense, the heartbeat of its pages:
including Bert, Nick, Pinky, Gos, Mince, Grinke, and Jimmy
– and to all North Enders, past, present and future.
Most of all, though, I dedicate Markings to my wife Vivian,
a very special North Ender who has been my partner in putting this book together,
and my partner in life for thirty-six wonderful years.

- A. J. Paquette

Production

Texts and compilation copyright © 1995
by Loch & Mayberry Fine Art Inc.
Artwork copyright © 1995 by A.J. Paquette

Published by Loch & Mayberry Fine Art Inc.
306 St. Mary's Road, Winnipeg, Manitoba
Canada R2M 1J8

Book and Cover Design:
Gary R.S. Styrchak

Production Assistance and Editorial:
Glen Gore-Smith

Printed and bound in Canada by Friesens
Altona, Manitoba, Canada R0G 0B0

Copyright

Canadian Cataloguing in Publication Data

Paquette, A. J., 1930–

Markings

ISBN 1–55056–400–5

1. North End (Winnipeg, Man.) – Pictorial works.
2. North End (Winnipeg, Man.) – History.
3. Winnipeg (Man.) – Pictorial works. 4. Winnipeg (Man.) – History. I. Title

FC3396.37.P36 1995 971.27'43 C95–920216–1
F1064.5.W7P36 1995

First printing, October 1995
Printed in Canada on acid-free paper

Acknowledgements

Bill Mayberry

Markings: Scenes and Recollections of Winnipeg's North End was more than two years in the making, and I am happy to have this chance to credit the many people who helped turn the book from a concept into a reality:

Thanks to Armand and Vivian Paquette, for having the perseverance and dedication (not to mention almost heroic stamina) to research, create and nurture *Markings* through to completion.

Thanks to Monty Hall for so graciously sharing his reflections on the North End in the introduction to the book.

Thanks to Tom Olenick, Leo Mol and Luther Pokrant, who generously contributed introductions to the individual sections.

Thanks to Peter Liba, for his invaluable interest and support of this project in its initial stages.

I also wish to thank the people who toiled with such dedication on the project and publication: Gary Styrchak and Glen Gore-Smith, for design, format concept, layout, and editorial work; and Friesens for production and printing.

Finally, a special acknowledgement and thank you to the many friends and clients who have supported the art work of A.J. Paquette, and the Loch & Mayberry Gallery, for more than twenty years.

Contents

“The North End, historically, began as you moved in a northerly direction through the subway at Higgins and Main. As you came out of the tunnel, you entered the North End, which lasted until somewhere around Matheson Avenue. After that, you were in the Kildonans. The North End was bordered by the Red River on the east side, and when you reached McPhillips Street you had gone about as far west as you could.”

- Monty Hall

Monty Hall

Certain places in North America are known for evoking strong reflections of nostalgia and pride: Just listen to the kids from Brooklyn, the Bronx or the Southside of Philadelphia talk about their old neighbourhoods. I don't recall anybody talking that way about the South End of Winnipeg – or the East End, or the West End. But when you hear somebody say they're a North Ender, you know what they mean.

At a reunion honouring the seventy-fifth anniversary of St. John's Technical High School several years back, we heard a recitation of all the famous doctors, lawyers, athletes and others who hailed from the North End. They included three Metropolitan Opera singers, a lawyer who sat on the World Court, the doctor who invented the heart-lung machine, and a famous nuclear scientist. We also produced a Chief Justice of the Supreme Court of Canada, along with countless show business personalities and hockey players.

The 4,500 people who came to that reunion from all parts of the world showed great pride in the city from which we came and great pride in the area from which we hailed: the North End.

My earliest recollections of the area date from when I lived in my grandparents' home on Hallet Street. We lived there with six of my mother's brothers and sisters, my grandparents and two of my great-grandparents. My other two great-grandparents lived on Euclid Avenue.

In its heyday, Hallet Street must have been important, because it housed Premier Norquay. By the time I lived there, however, it was a lower to lower middle-class microcosm of the North End. Although it was only a couple of hundred yards long, Hallet Street had

Ukrainian, Jewish, German, Polish and Chinese residents, as well as a couple of Anglo-Saxon families.

It was a melting pot, and yet we didn't quite melt. Our pot contained too many ingredients that didn't mix. People today intermingle much more, through social interaction, intermarriage, the mercantile world, and so on. But in those days we pretty much stayed to ourselves. This kind of Balkanization of a small midwestern city was not uncommon back then.

One thing we had in common, though, was the Depression. It tied people together – including merchants and their customers. My grandfather had a little butcher shop. There was a German tinsmith next door. Across the road there was a grocery store which was owned by an Anglo-Saxon. A shoe store, a dress shop and other little stores dotted the area, and there was one supermarket which challenged all the mom and pop stores on the street.

Yet customers kept these mom and pop stores going. Patrons knew that they and the shopkeepers were going through a kindred economic struggle, and there was a feeling of comradeship amongst the merchants, too. I remember my father turning to the German tinsmith next door for help in a crisis. If the grocer needed a parcel delivered to a far-off area, he would ask my father if he would mind, when he delivered his meat, taking the grocery parcel as well. So, although we didn't socialize, we had this mutual respect, because we were all trying to scratch out a living, working sixty and seventy-two hour weeks to survive.

For entertainment, we played games on streets or in school grounds. We'd look for an empty lot to play football and baseball in summer. In winter, we would carve our own rink on the river bank. If you looked up and down the Red River, you could see countless areas cleared off for skating and hockey rinks – areas each group claimed as its own.

If the river wasn't frozen over, we would wait for snow to turn the streets hard and ice-like. Occasionally, we would go to Drewry's, a brewery on the northeast corner of Redwood and Main, with a large skating rink on its grounds. The Drewry's rink had an enclosed hut where you could change skates and warm up before venturing out in the sub-zero weather. And that was about it for winter entertainment.

As a city, we were very influenced by the Depression and the climate, and our isolation from other urban centres. We were about five hundred miles from Minneapolis to the south; more than a thousand miles from Toronto in the east; and about the same distance from Vancouver to the west.

I believe that Winnipeggers were stronger for having to contend with economic hardship, the weather and the isolation. Maybe that's why Winnipeg produced more famous people per capita than any other community I can think of – and why the North End produced more than its share of eminent people.

Former Winnipegger Monty Hall is a well-known television personality and philanthropist.

Introduction by Tom Olenick

I bought my first Paquette painting in the early Seventies. It was a scene of an old, abandoned farm building on McPhillips Street, painted in May of 1970.

The opening for his show was held in a furniture store on Portage Avenue West. I don't recall the name of the store, but it felt very strange to look at paintings and meet an artist, surrounded by kitchen sets, lamps and chesterfields.

Our first conversation confirmed my impression that Armand Paquette's works should be purchased and followed as he developed into a mature artist. This I have done and I continue to receive pleasure from a number of his paintings I have since acquired – not only for myself, but also for my children.

In his 1870s *Lectures on Art*, John Ruskin said, "The function of art is the recording of fact" and further, that "giving brightness to the picture is much, but giving brightness to life is more."

This is what Armand Paquette does well. His portrayal of historic scenes is vividly painted with a discipline and a devotion to the vintage North End. It will always bring to the viewer an intense nostalgia that will make it almost impossible to put this book aside.

Art collector Tom Olenick, a semi-retired business executive, is a University of Manitoba graduate. Olenick was a Human Rights Commissioner for Manitoba from 1975 to the beginning of 1982.

Royal Alex From the Subway

Passing into the North End from the subway was like emerging into another city, distinct from the rest of Winnipeg. This area had a heavy concentration of East Europeans, Jews, Slavs and a good mix of other ethnic groups. And they all brought their unique customs with them. A lot of back porches had sauerkraut and garlicky dill pickles brewing in barrels and crocks. This was the part of town where "outsiders" were introduced to perogies, holobchi, gefilte fish and many other mouth-watering foods.

ROYAL ALEX FROM THE SUBWAY 1992
Alkyd, 22 x 30
Collection of Ken and Betty Sutherland
Winnipeg, Manitoba

WHITLA & CO

The New Arrivals

In the early part of the century, when you left your home country, you usually left everything behind for good. You couldn't exactly hop a jet across the ocean for the holidays. So I've often wondered what it must have been like for people to have to leave their families, friends and homeland and travel thousands of miles to a young, raw country, to start all over again from scratch. When or if family or friends renewed contact, the emotions must have been overwhelming. The area shown here is the New Jerusalem on a soggy, foggy morning when families are reunited after a long absence.

THE NEW ARRIVALS 1995
Alkyd, 18 x 24
Collection of Friesens Corporation
Altona, Manitoba

North End Market, 1910

The Farmers Market was on Main Street, between Stella and Flora. It was a busy, colourful place for many decades. But by the Sixties, it was almost forsaken by tradesmen, and few people strayed in through its gate. The last vendor we saw there was a fellow selling rabbits and a bit of produce. Some say that the supermarkets were to blame for the market's downfall. But an informed source who goes by the nickname of Mince tells a different story. He says that the Farmers Market did well as long as the property it was on belonged to the fellow who had Smitty's Fish & Chips, nearby. Old man Smitty gave the vendors a real break on the rent, which allowed them to make a buck. After Smitty passed away in the mid-Fifties, his widow sold the property to the City and moved to the States. Naturally, the City hiked the rents, which put the squeeze on the tradespeople. And, according to Mince, that was what spelled the end of the Farmers Market. Attempts to get another market going, further north on Main, and later over on Regent Street, fared poorly for the same reason: the rental costs were too high.

OLD NORTH END MARKET 1993
Alkyd, 12 x 16
Collection of the Manitoba Telephone System
Winnipeg, Manitoba

The New Jerusalem

At the turn of the century, the area just north of the CP rail yards was called the New Jerusalem. The name may have come because of the heavy concentration of Jewish immigrants, including Hassidim, in the area. Or perhaps it was called the New Jerusalem because this new world was relatively free, after the hardships, bigotry and congestion of the old countries. Many of these immigrants were extremely poor and constructed dwellings of used lumber, or added on to existing buildings.

THE NEW JERUSALEM 1994
Alkyd, 18 x 24
Collection of Mindel and Tom Olenick
Winnipeg, Manitoba

TEL DUFFERIN

Evening at the Royal Alex

This historic landmark, a Canadian Pacific Railway hotel, had a beautiful foyer with huge murals. The Alex was often patronized by important personages, including royalty. Speaking of important personages, a friend of mine's stepmother went to a wedding at the Royal Alex and made off with a keg of beer. I don't know how she managed it, but there's a good chance she was in cahoots with a cabby. Anyway, she took off and vanished (keg and all). A little more than a week later, she called home from her sister's place. I understand this lady was a bit of a souse.

EVENING AT THE ROYAL ALEX 1991
Alkyd, 16 x 24
Collection of John and Bonnie Buhler
Winnipeg, Manitoba

DRUGS
JOVAL

Rainstorm North Main

Bert's dad passed on his old Model T to Bert. We drove around the North End, whistling at girls and wisecracking with them. One bright, sunny day, the sky seemed to cloud over black, as if by magic. Then the rain came down hard, sending people scurrying for shelter in doorways and under store awnings. Of course, some people are always prepared and have their umbrellas with them at all times, in case of such an eventuality. Bert was always prepared, too. Anyway, the old car came to a sputtering halt in that heavy rain. Bert hauled out a pair of pliers and a bicycle pump. Then he got out of the car, tinkered under the hood with his gear and fixed the problem – just as his papa had taught him.

RAINSTORM NORTH MAIN 1994
Alkyd, 18 x 24
Collection of the College of Physicians and Surgeons
Winnipeg, Manitoba

Feathers

Old Mrs. Kowalki barely knew a word of English, so she spoke to us in Ukrainian. She smiled and gestured a lot. We couldn't understand her, but we liked to visit with her anyway, because the things she did were always interesting and mysterious to us. One of those things was decapitating and plucking chickens. She needed a tub of boiling-hot water to scald the chicken so that she could pluck the feathers. She needed another hot tub for the feathers, which she used in making pillows. It was always fascinating for us kids to watch the chickens being defeathered, even though the aroma was a little hard to take.

FEATHERS 1992
Alkyd, 12 x 16
Collection of Mr. and Mrs. Jim Gauthier
Winnipeg, Manitoba

Rag Man

There wasn't a lot of money floating around in our neighbourhood. Weekly allowances were unheard-of and "spending money" was a rarity. So we scoured the alleys for liquor bottles and searched the garbage cans for whatever else might be saleable. We'd hoard this loot until the Rag Man made his rounds. The Rag Man always wore a suit and tie, and a fedora or a straw hat. He was a very pleasant old man with a dry sense of humour – most of which went right over our heads. He'd sort out our junk and pay us for what he wanted. He always took the booze bottles, including wine bottles. Since the bootleggers wouldn't take wine bottles, we preferred to do business with the Rag Man.

RAG MAN 1992
Alkyd, 15 x 22
Collection of Mr. and Mrs. Ken Bishop
Winnipeg, Manitoba

The Farmer's Market

Walter, one of our friends, who originally hailed from Teulon, had an uncle who ran a booth at the Farmers Market on Stella and Main. We'd go to see him in the hopes of getting something good to eat, but all he ever gave us were scrawny little potatoes.

The Farmers Market was, for all intents and purposes, an outdoor supermarket. You could get dairy products, poultry, vegetables and some grain there. We liked to go because it was so vibrant and alive. Trucks were being unloaded, farmers toted their produce to their booths, dodging in and out of the congestion in the process. You could always spot wise old ladies haggling over prices they invariably found too steep. Younger people usually lacked the spirit or the experience to barter.

An old farmer I met many years after the market closed told me an interesting tale about selling chickens. He said, "I decided to be very honest when I began selling chickens there. So when people asked what I was selling, I told them roosters. But they wanted hens, so, eventually, I decided to be dishonest. When they asked what I was selling, I asked them what they wanted. When they said 'hens,' I told them 'that's what I got.' And then they bought."

THE FARMER'S MARKET 1994
Alkyd, 18 x 24
Collection of Dr. and Mrs. R. Noble
Butte, Montana

Back Lane Barter

The Rag Man (I believe Mr. Kratebergh was his name) was a great talker. He enjoyed telling tales about his emigration from Eastern Europe, and how he and his family came here with nothing but the clothing on their backs. When he started his business, he had only a pushcart. He walked the streets and alleys, buying used and broken items that people no longer needed. By reselling these items, the Rag Man eventually earned enough money to buy a horse and wagon which made life a lot easier – and more productive – for him. With a twinkle in his eyes, he'd say, "Mine is a rags to riches story." This was a man who liked his own humour.

BACK LANE BARTER 1995
Alkyd, 18 x 24
Collection of Loch & Mayberry Fine Art Inc.
Winnipeg, Manitoba

The Ice Man

There weren't many refrigerators back in the Thirties and Forties, but there were a lot of ice boxes. The Ice Man made his rounds weekly, replenishing melted ice for twenty-five cents a block. He drove a team of horses and a flatbed wagon which contained blocks of ice covered with heavy tarpaulin. His was a tough job: he often had to climb three flights of outside stairs to deliver the ice. We usually got the shiest kid (with some pushing and shoving, of course) to ask the ice man for free pieces of broken ice. It worked best that way, because the ice man always liked to tease a bit. I skipped school sometimes to ride around with him.

THE ICE MAN 1993
Alkyd, 18 x 24
Collection of Mr. and Mrs. Wes Hull
Winnipeg, Manitoba

Mobile Market Garden

In late summer and early fall, farmers would drive down our streets, their trucks laden with fresh produce. They had only to knock on one or two doors before the whole neighbourhood knew they were there: the kids spread the word. The farmers came bearing sacks of potatoes, plus boxes heaped with cabbage, beets, corn and onions. They brought beans and peas in paper bags. And corn on the cob, which was what we kids were anticipating with great delight. Some of us could barely wait to savour our first taste of corn on the cob.

MOBILE MARKET GARDEN 1992
Alkyd, 15 x 22
Collection of Ken and Betty Sutherland
Winnipeg, Manitoba

Chicken Delight

Many backyards had chickens running loose behind wire fences. During the summer, eggs were collected from the laying hens. Come autumn, these hens were served up, one by one, at Sunday dinners. This must have been in appreciation of their egg-laying labours. Kids playing in the yard too close to the wire fence, would sometimes inadvertently set the chickens free. And then the action started, with chickens running amok in the lane, kids chasing after them, and adults screaming holy retribution at the kids.

CHICKEN DELIGHT 1992
Alkyd, 15 x 22
Collection of the Government of Manitoba
Winnipeg, Manitoba

Bicycle/Tricycle Race

Kids are always involved in competitive games. The east side of Main Street is almost ideal for bicycle racing, because the land slopes down to the Red River. This scene shows two brothers and a buddy, who staged a race in 1954. The friend wiped out almost from the start, making this strictly a family affair.

BICYCLE/TRICYCLE RACE 1994
Alkyd, 15 x 22
Collection of Piston Ring Service
Winnipeg, Manitoba

PISTON RING
SERVICE SUPP
DC1-388

Chicken Feed

Chickens were usually baba's responsibility. She fed, butchered and defeathered them. The feathers were later used for making pillows and comforters. And talk about recycling: flour sacks and sugar bags were even made into pillow slips! Of course, they had to be bleached, because of their coloured print.

CHICKEN FEED 1991
Alkyd, 12 x 16
Collection of Mr. and Mrs. Ken Bishop
Winnipeg, Manitoba

Caught in The Act

During the Second World War, when we were in our early teens, garden raiding was a very popular pastime with us. We never quite saw this as theft: We liked to pretend we were on commando raids, like some of our war heroes. Sometimes it was a close call – especially if we were surprised by a dog, or by someone who had been raided once too often (we had competition). Those were the years the government was promoting Victory Gardens. The idea was for people to grow as much of their own food as possible, so that there would be enough canned and other commercial food, for our soldiers overseas. With this in mind, some of the other kids accused us of being unpatriotic – but they never hesitated to ask for a share of the spoils, which were generally potatoes, carrots or peas.

CAUGHT IN THE ACT 1992
Alkyd, 12 x 16
Collection of Mr. and Mrs. Rob Woodley
Winnipeg, Manitoba

Potato Roast

Roasting potatoes on an open fire in a friend's back yard could be a great deal of fun. Most of the time, they came out charred black on the outside and half-raw in the centre. Nonetheless, we ate them and extolled their gourmet quality (I think we were all lying). The potatoes were usually swiped from someone else's garden, anyway.

POTATO ROAST 1994
Alkyd, 18 x 24
Collection of the Government of Manitoba
Winnipeg, Manitoba

Moving Day

In the 1950s, I worked for Crescent Moving and Storage for a while. I often worked with a fellow whom I can only remember as Mike. He was a powerful man, and liked to carry heavy appliances such as stoves and washing machines by himself. I was a 135-pound weakling and (of course) tried to hold my own – a very exhausting business. Some of the people we moved would feel sorry for me doing all that heavy work, and would suggest that I sit down and let the big guys do the heavy lifting.

On one of our jobs – a third-floor outdoor stairs affair of a kind we got all too frequently – the old man we were moving kept stopping us on the stairs just to tell us a joke. Naturally, he'd do this when we were struggling with a particularly heavy item, such as a fridge. The worst part of it all was that I never did like heights.

MOVING DAY 1993
Alkyd, 18 x 24
Collection of Bruce and Monica Ransom
Winnipeg, Manitoba

Willow Whistles

On Pritchard Avenue near Arlington, there was an old fellow who sat on his porch all summer long. He'd have lengths of willow in a bucket of water beside his chair. To entertain us whenever we came, he made willow whistles for us. He was usually a little boozy and mellow. He'd tell stories about the old country and his youth, while he whittled willow whistles. He'd cut a piece about six inches long. Then he'd take that piece and cut, skin-deep all around the circumference, about three-quarters from the end. After that, he'd cut a notch in the short end. His next step was to tap the centre cylinder loose from the bark and hollow out just enough of the stem to allow for an air passage. Finally, he'd replace the cylinder – and a whistle was born.

WILLOW WHISTLES 1993
Alkyd, 12 x 16
Collection of Loch & Mayberry Fine Art Inc.
Winnipeg, Manitoba

Crazy Quilt

Quilting was more than a hobby or a craft in the Thirties and Forties. It was a necessity for people who could not afford the luxury of new blankets. In those days, people used material left over from other sewing. Remnants of old clothing and other materials were put aside for months or even years, until there was enough fabric to make a new quilt. A "Crazy Quilt" pattern used the scrap material more or less in the shape it came in, rather than cutting it to fit a geometric pattern. There was even less waste that way. Crazy Quilts were stitched together piece by piece – a laborious task, requiring many long hours, often in poor lighting.

Daughters in the family would have the opportunity to use some fabric pieces for their dolls' blankets. When visitors arrived, tea was served and the work in progress was brought out. The ensuing technical discussion could use up the better part of an afternoon.

CRAZY QUILT 1994
Alkyd, 12 x 16
Collection of Loch & Mayberry Fine Art Inc.
Winnipeg, Manitoba

Kelekis Chips

The Kelekis business began with a pushcart, featuring peanuts and popcorn. Chips came soon after. After the movies, it was almost a must for adults and children to stop at Kelekis for a Coke and chips (that's what we used to call french fries). It was a most popular place to dine and socialize before or after going on to other business. Today, it's still a popular restaurant – and something of a landmark. It's still famous for its chips. And it still has a takeout window.

KELEKIS CHIPS 1994
Alkyd, 15 x 22
Collection of Loch & Mayberry Fine Art Inc.
Winnipeg, Manitoba

CHIPS
ICE COLD
CHIPS

Midnight Special to Winnipeg Beach

The Saturday train to Winnipeg Beach left the CP station at the Royal Alex around noon and returned at midnight. It was a bit noisy on the way to the beach, with lots of laughing and horseplay. But the return trip was bedlam. The coaches were antiques and still had gaslights. The floors were slatted and the seats were of some sort of braided material not unlike wicker. The conductor and trainman came through on the return trip and lit the lamps. And shortly after they passed through the coach, the younger kids – who'd been bribed by the older ones – extinguished them. I made some loot that way. There was plenty of necking and drinking going on among the older kids. Fights often broke out, as well. It must have been a punishment run for the train staff.

THE MIDNIGHT SPECIAL TO WINNIPEG BEACH 1994
Alkyd, 15 x 22
Collection of Johnston Group (Benefit Plan) Inc.
Winnipeg, Manitoba

2815
2815

Autumn, Isaac Newton

In room nineteen, our homeroom at Isaac Newton, this big fellow who went by the name of Gos would lumber into class every morning and ask us, "Who's boss?" The answer from the rest of the class was always, "Gos is boss." There was another fellow in class who biked in from Brooklands and who was usually late, for which he always got a dressing-down from Miss Chislett, our homeroom teacher. I can't remember his name, except that it was Scottish. At any rate, he always wore a kind of vacant smile, which served to aggravate both Miss Chislett and Gos. Naturally, Gos took every opportunity to badger the fellow. And this kid merely smiled, until one day when he came in looking a bit out of sorts. Gos, of course, started needling him – for the last time, as it turned out. The kid from Brooklands was a little short, but well built. He leaped out of his seat and smeared Gos.

AUTUMN, ISAAC NEWTON 1994
Alkyd, 22 x 30
Collection of Loch & Mayberry Fine Art Inc.
Winnipeg, Manitoba

All Hallow's Eve

When Halloween arrived, we would take our mother's pillow case and go around the neighbourhood for Halloween apples. And in those days, most goodies were just that: apples. Candy was a real treat. We would yell "trick or treat" and we'd usually have to sing to get our treat. Many of the kids were a little mischievous. We would be out until all hours, but it seemed that our parents didn't have to worry much about our safety in those days.

ALL HALLOW'S EVE 1993
Alkyd, 18 x 24
Collection of Mr. and Mrs. John Scurfield
Winnipeg, Manitoba

ANNE'S GROCERY
ANNE'S GROCERY

Window Shopping

There was a sports shop on Arlington Street where Nick, a friend of mine, used to stop and price the hockey shirts every time we passed by. He was saving some of his paper route money to buy a Maple Leafs sweater. They were his favourite team and he hoped to play for them one day. However, Nick wasn't much of a hockey player and he wound up running a corner grocery store.

WINDOW SHOPPING 1990
Alkyd, 18 x 24
Collection of Mr. Bill Ryall
Winnipeg, Manitoba

SKATES
SHARPENED
10¢
FREE PRESS

Blocking Traffic

Back alleys were generally the kids' domain. Actually, the whole outdoors was the kids' domain. Adults merely used back alleys to get from point A to point B, while kids played all kinds of games there – including hockey, kick the can, hide and seek, cricket and hippy-tippy. Of course, which game we played depended on the season. And, naturally, no one was in much of a hurry to make way for not-too-patient drivers. Kids pretended not to notice the car, and this usually drew a burst of foul language from the driver, as well as a raucous blast from the horn.

BLOCKING TRAFFIC 1992
Alkyd, 15 x 22
Collection of MacDonald Auto Body Ltd.
Winnipeg, Manitoba

St. John's College

The old St. John's College was situated on Main and Cathedral. The school had its roots in the Red River Academy, founded in 1820 by the Anglican Church to teach the kids of Hudson's Bay Company employees, and Natives. St. John's itself came into being in 1866. In my day, it seemed to be something of an island unto itself, like England, perched off the coast of Europe. My pals and I didn't pay much attention to it – except during the war and in wintertime. It would have been hard not to notice those cadets parading around the school grounds. Of course, other schools had army cadets, but the fellows at St. John's were the only ones I saw who actually had uniforms. The campus building itself came in handy during the winters. We'd use the school walls for shelter on cold, blustery evenings when we were en route to the Olympic Stadium. We would go there to root for our buddies at junior hockey games. St. John's College and the Olympic Stadium came down in the late Fifties, as I recall. An apartment went up where the Olympic used to be, and St. John's moved out to a beautiful building on the University of Manitoba campus in 1958.

ST. JOHN'S COLLEGE 1994
Alkyd, 22 x 30
Collection of St. John's-Ravenscourt
Alumni Association
Winnipeg, Manitoba

A.J.Paquette

Morning Papers

I was fourteen when I got a route for the now-defunct Winnipeg Tribune. My goal was to make enough money to buy a small printing press and some art supplies. But I hadn't reckoned on subscribers who dodged payment – or who sent in complaints, for which I'd be fined. There was one family in an apartment block from whom I had been trying to collect for some time. When I was knocking on their door, a man from a neighbouring suite told me that those people were away on holidays. Naturally, I didn't leave a paper there that day. And (naturally) when I went to pick up my papers the next day, there was a pink slip waiting for me. This meant a fine. I tried to explain, but I still had to pay the fine. When a customer didn't pay, it came out of the paperboy's pocket. So I quit after a month, and took work Saturdays in a coal yard, filling bags with coal. It was tough, but I earned more in four hours than I did in two weeks delivering papers – with none of the headaches.

MORNING PAPERS 1990
Alkyd, 20 x 24
Collection of Mr. Graeme D. Sifton
Winnipeg, Manitoba

The Castle

We lived just down the street from this house, on College Avenue. It was dubbed "The Castle" because of its architectural style, which is quite a mix, and because of the turret on the northwest corner. This house was a popular attraction. I never met or knew the people who lived in the Castle, so it was always a rather pleasant, vaguely Gothic, mystery, and it remains so to this day. Which is, in my opinion, the way it should be.

THE CASTLE 1994
Alkyd, 12 x 16
Collection of MacDonald Auto Body Ltd.
Winnipeg, Manitoba

Back Yard Rink

Having a backyard rink could make a kid very popular in the neighbourhood, something like having a swimming pool would today. These rinks were great for practising stick-handling and dreaming of NHL stardom. But when things got too crowded and noisy, the kids were usually sent packing by an irate parent, who usually threw in a lecture about proper behaviour.

BACK YARD RINK 1994
Alkyd, 14 x 20
Collection of Midland Walwyn Capital Inc.
Winnipeg, Manitoba

Just Being Kids

From the Salter Bridge west, the aged houses on Jarvis were being demolished to make way for "redevelopment." The first to go were the ones facing the bridge. A heap of rubble remained for quite some time, and with the winter snow, it became a slide for neighbourhood kids. Personally, I was sorry to see the street go. The back alley, in particular, was quite colourful, with fences of time-darkened lumber reinforced with Coca-Cola, Seven-Up and other signs. One fence had a bedspring filling a gap. Some yards had an accumulation of treasures collected over the years – such as tubs, wringer washing machines and lumber, along with a great number of etceteras.

JUST BEING KIDS 1993
Alkyd, 12 x 16
Collection of Mr. and Mrs. Ken Bishop
Winnipeg, Manitoba

The Snow Bank

Using cardboard for sleds on our makeshift slides was a favourite pastime. Low sheds and deep snow also made for a good opportunity to play king of the castle. As a game progressed, it generally got rougher, and the girls were just as guilty as the boys of foul play. They were often more 'enthusiastic' than the boys, except that – when push came to shove – they were always using their gender as an excuse not to be treated roughly.

On a winter day three or four years ago, we were driving down Pritchard Avenue. The snow was banked up high on the boulevards, and the kids were doing exactly what we did when we were their age. They were sliding down the banks on pieces of cardboard that were probably pulled out of a neighbour's garage, creating a mess in the process. Some things never change, I guess.

THE SNOW BANK 1994
Alkyd, 15 x 22
Collection of Mr. Andrew Ogaranko, Q.C.
Winnipeg, Manitoba

Late for the Game

After World War II, jobs were more plentiful and paid a little more. People had some money in their pockets – not enough to buy a new car, but usually enough for an older model. There were still a lot of Model A's and T's around, along with rarer autos such as the Whippet and the Essex. The specialized tires we have today weren't around then. Chains were the usual winter dress for tires. Cars that didn't sport chains on their tires slipped and slid on the ice, or got hung up on snowbanks. This used to happen on our street, right where we played hockey. So we had to put the game on hold until we had helped extricate the unlucky car from our "rink."

LATE FOR THE GAME 1992
Alkyd, 15 x 22
Collection of McMahon Canada
Winnipeg, Manitoba

Late Night Shopping, Selkirk Avenue

During the Christmas season, Selkirk Avenue was a busy thoroughfare. Oretzki's, Woolworth's, the Palace Theatre, the Merchants Hotel, plus many restaurants and other shops did a brisk trade. Next door to the Palace Theatre (when it was still operating) was a pool room with a shoeshine stand. There were a couple of other shoeshine shops and a novelty store which, rumour had it, were actually fronts for bookie joints. The display in the novelty shop window was covered with a thick layer of dust but this establishment was still open for business. Circumstantial evidence, I grant you.

LATE NIGHT SHOPPING, SELKIRK AVE. 1993
Alkyd, 24 x 36
Collection of Zipper Transportation Services Ltd.
Winnipeg, Manitoba

PALACE
ORETZKIS
DEPT. STORE LTD
AFRICAN QUEEN
TAXI

Wish List

A window arrayed with toys stops kids in their tracks every time. Despite shouts from their parents urging them to hurry along, it takes a long time for the kids to pull themselves away from the display. And, when they finally get moving, they do so with great reluctance.

WISH LIST 1994
Alkyd, 12 x 16
Collection of David and Alison Loch
Winnipeg, Manitoba

Twelve Days of Christmas

Many families waited until Christmas Eve to buy their trees so they could get them at clearance prices. Of course, the best trees had been picked by then, and the ones that were left were rather scraggly. And, as the kids dragged them home along the sidewalks, the trees lost even more limbs and needles. But some artful decorating worked miracles and got everyone into the spirit of the season.

The days leading up to Christmas are often pretty busy. Gifts are purchased, cards sent out, the house and tree are decorated and the baking is done for the Yuletide feast. This hectic, yet enjoyable time of preparation always put me in mind of the song, "The Twelve Days of Christmas."

TWELVE DAYS OF CHRISTMAS 1993
Alkyd, 14 x 21
Collection of Tribaron Holdings
Toronto, Ontario

CLOSED
X-MAS

Here We Come A'Caroling

Caroling is one of the most charming Christmas traditions we have. The pastor of the Baptist church used to lead a group of young people from house to house in our area, chanting the familiar carols. This gave Christmas a very special warmth, despite the below zero temperatures.

HERE WE COME A'CAROLING 1995
Alkyd, 15 x 22
Collection of Loch & Mayberry Fine Art Inc.
Winnipeg, Manitoba

Bob Skates

Bob skates are just like miniature bobsleds, strapped to the boots. They are starter skates for little children, who always need a volunteer to help them stay on their feet. These skates were more often used on icy streets and sidewalks than on rinks – unless there was a backyard rink in the neighbourhood.

BOB SKATES 1992
Alkyd, 12 x 16
Collection of Mr. Tammas R. Scott
Winnipeg, Manitoba

Make Believe and Reality

Arthur Grinke's (pronounced Gring-kee) uncle had left an ancient Ford coupe in Arthur's backyard. It had no tires, so it was up on blocks. Many's the time we would sit in that car for hours, daydreaming about the great things we would do someday. Or we'd play cops and robbers, pretending that the old coupe was a police car. We would get so engrossed in our game, we wouldn't notice that some of our other friends (who were as mischievous as we were) had come by to add to the action. We left ourselves wide open for a snowball attack – from ambush, of course. Opportunities such as this were hard for other kids to pass up.

MAKE BELIEVE AND REALITY 1992
Alkyd, 15 x 22
Collection of McMahon Canada
Winnipeg, Manitoba

A.J.Paquette

Tire Swing

Jimmy's dad put a tire swing up for the neighbourhood kids. It was one of the few yards we were allowed to play in. We built a gang shack against the fence and formed a club which lasted for a couple of hours, because we couldn't agree on who would hold what position. However, that didn't stop us from using the shack as a fort, a pirate ship or whatever else crossed our minds. In winter we used it to launch ourselves into the snowbanks off the swing. We got good height and distance. It was scary, but fun.

You might say that Jimmy was a dangerous practical joker. He once attempted to burn the shack down while some of us were in it. And then there was the time that his brother Jack bought an old Chevy. Jimmy asked my brother if he'd like to try the car out. Naturally, Jimmy didn't tell him that the brakes were shot. So my brother ran into Jimmy's back porch, wreaking a considerable amount of damage. Jimmy wanted to be called Pinky. I don't know why, except that it may have had something to do with one of his movie heroes.

TIRE SWING 1989
Alkyd, 24 x 36
Collection of Bill and Joan Mayberry
Winnipeg, Manitoba

North End Weekend

Our neighbourhood challenge games of street hockey frequently turned into brawls. Home street pride demanded that you win whatever way worked best. We all knew this meant that back alley rules applied when the game wasn't proceeding according to plan, i.e. when you weren't winning.

NORTH END WEEKEND 1992
Alkyd, 15 x 22
Collection of Mr. and Mrs. Mutschel
Thompson, Manitoba

A.J. Paquette

Going Nowhere, Main and Redwood

It was a mild day for March, and the snow came down wet and heavy. The streets were treacherous and next to impossible to navigate. As the snow got deeper, the cars slid until they became hung up and immobilized, with their wheels spinning.

GOING NOWHERE, MAIN AND REDWOOD 1993
Alkyd, 22 x 30
Collection of Mr. and Mrs. Jim Gauthier
Winnipeg, Manitoba

March Storm of '66

The 1966 storm was in a class of its own, even for Winnipeg. As I recall, the city practically shut down for two or three days while we dug ourselves out. You might say it was a major inconvenience, but – admit it or not – our heavy snowstorms can also be exciting. Kids get to take a holiday from school and adults have an excuse to be late for work – or maybe not show up at all. We also get to be good Samaritans, helping one another out of storm-caused difficulties, with a mood of camaraderie pervading.

MARCH STORM OF '66 1993
Alkyd, 24 x 36
Collection of MacDonald Auto Body Ltd.
Winnipeg, Manitoba

ADA
A.J.Paquette

St. John's Tec

A lot of famous people call St. John's Tec their alma mater, including Monty Hall, Burton Cummings and Larry Zolf. In fact, more celebrities probably went there than any other school in Winnipeg. I went there once a week for shops, and I guess you could say that I was in a league of my own.

I was pretty bad at woodwork. The shops teacher used to laugh behind my back and show my work to the other kids to get a rise out of the class. He even took my stuff on tour to some other class rooms. As a result, a couple of teachers came to our classroom door to take a look at me.

ST. JOHN'S TEC 1994
Alkyd, 22 x 30
Collection of Miss Ollie H. Landega
Winnipeg, Manitoba

Spring Rain, Luxton School

Luxton Elementary School is in a pleasantly secluded area on the east side of Main Street. On this wet spring day, some of the kids are being escorted to school under umbrellas by their moms. The kids on their own get to play in the water which is running in the gutter.

Monty Hall and Burton Cummings, among other well-known personalities, attended Luxton School before moving on to St. John's Tec.

SPRING RAIN, LUXTON SCHOOL 1993
Alkyd, 22 x 30
Collection of Loch & Mayberry Fine Art Inc.
Winnipeg, Manitoba

Vivian's House

This is Vivian's house, where my wife lived when she was a kid. I didn't know her at the time, and would never have guessed that we would end up being lifelong partners (thirty-six years as of the publication of this book). Anyway, Vivian lived here with her grandmother, mother, uncles, aunts and brothers. There were eleven in all. A lot of people could be put into a small house in those days. Before World War II, people mostly lived in rental houses. Privately-owned homes weren't as common then as they are now.

VIVIAN'S HOUSE 1993
Alkyd, 12 x 16
Collection of Mr. and Mrs. Ken Bishop
Winnipeg, Manitoba

Ukrainian Wedding

Except for the hairstyles and cars, this is a timeless scene, showing an old tradition lasting well on into the Eighties.

Weddings always have attracted onlookers, especially young girls and elderly people. This wedding is at the venerable St. Ivan Suchavsky Ukrainian Orthodox Cathedral on Main Street, directly across from Flora Avenue.

I don't know if they still sell perogies out of the basement at St. Ivan's, but my wife and I used to drop in and buy a few dozen every week, when we lived in Winnipeg. It was on Fridays, I think.

UKRAINIAN WEDDING 1995
Alkyd, 18 x 24
Collection of Miss Ollie H. Landega
Winnipeg, Manitoba

Introduction by Leo Mol

As a sculptor, I follow a long-established tradition which stresses the importance of the figure in art. It is my feeling that a portrait or figural work should reflect the inner character of a subject in such a way that the viewer has the impression of meeting a living person.

My colleague, Armand Paquette, is a keen observer of life. He has an intuition for character which is essential among figurative artists. His works in drawing, painting and sculpture clearly reflect his understanding of his subjects. Armand's work in bronze captures the human spirit with an energy that demonstrates his love of detail and his fascination with people.

One sculpture which stands out in my mind is *Bus Stop*. This grouping of several figures waiting for a bus depicts a situation we have all experienced. It's a picture we see every winter day, and yet Paquette portrays it as a poignant moment. In this scene, old people and young are braced against the cold wind, anticipating the arrival of the bus. He cleverly contrasts the attitude of the young and the old. The elderly ladies are bundled up warmly, while the teenagers stand in light jackets, trying to appear nonchalant.

Each of Paquette's sculptures shows a sensitivity to situations we encounter in our everyday lives. I can appreciate them as a sculptor and as a Winnipegger.

Leo Mol

Leo Mol is an internationally-renowned sculptor. His work is included in collections around the world, including those of the Vatican, the National Gallery of Canada, and the National Portrait Gallery in Washington, D.C.

Bus Stop

I'm always fascinated by what people do in a given situation – how they occupy their time. Take this small group of people waiting for a bus at the close of a working day. The teenagers at the end of the line are concentrating on each other. Adulation, I'd say. The workman's a little impatient to get home. You had a lot of working men in the North End in the old days. At the beginning of the line, there are two elderly ladies. The younger one is holding the other lady's arm, to balance her, while the other woman is bent over to put down her shopping bag. Action and reaction: I guess that's what everything is, isn't it?

BUS STOP 1993
Bronze, h. 13½ in.
Edition of 20

BUS

Snowball Wars

I always try to make a sculpture speak for itself. Here's a snowball fight, a tradition that still goes on today. A lot of the action in the old days took place in the back alleys – part of the great outdoors, which really is the kids domain. Alleys had buildings, fences, sheds and garbage cans, any or all of which were ideal for playing. These two kids are stationed beside a trash can, because of its potential for defense. The lid becomes a shield, something that goes way back to ancient times.

SNOWBALL WARS 1993
Bronze, h. 20 in.
Edition of 20

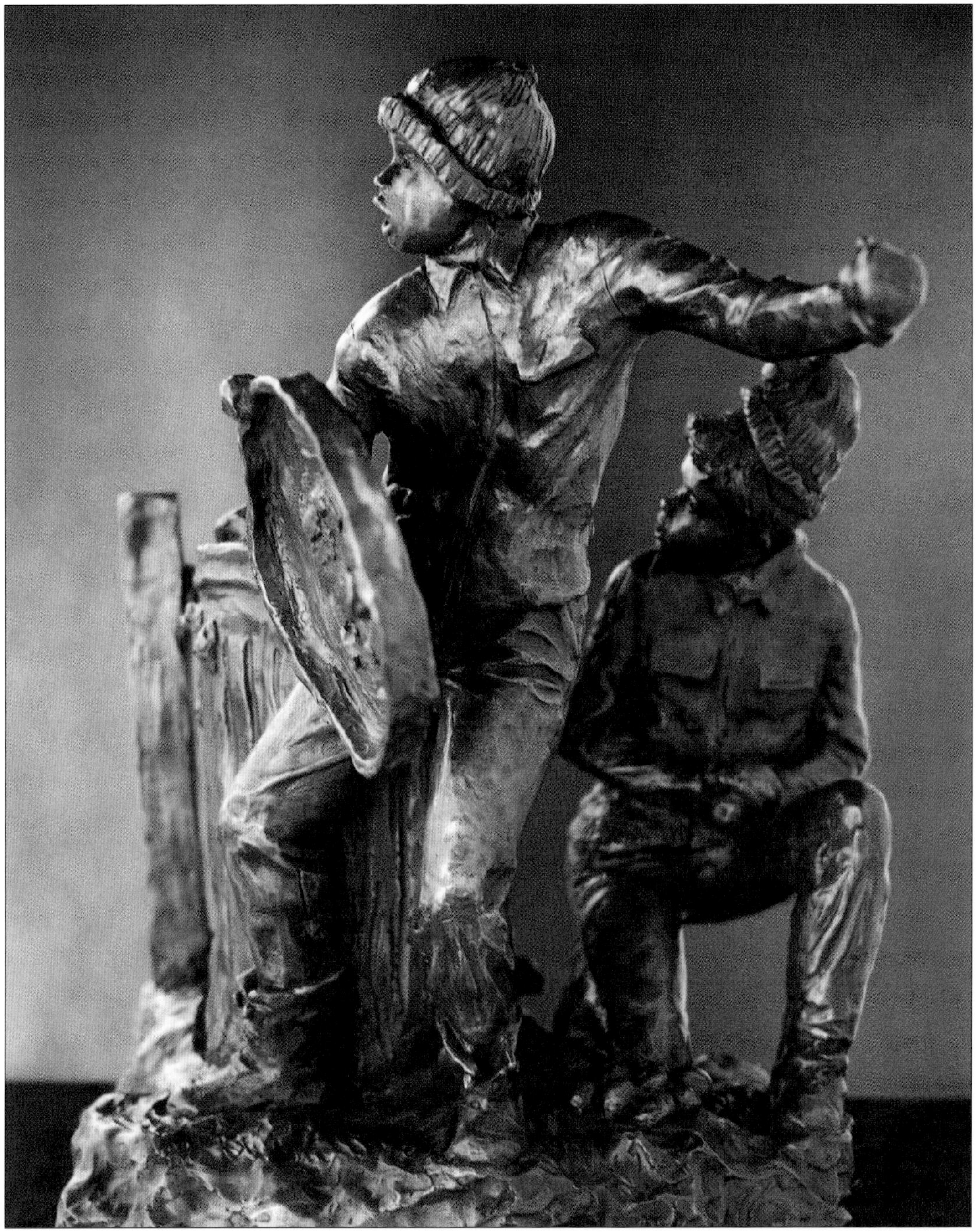

Potato Planting

Here's gidgi (grandfather) sowing potatoes and grumbling to himself while he does it. I got the idea that gidgis often grumbled to themselves, although they were usually very friendly. They'd often come over to the back alley fence and smile and chat with us, even though we didn't understand Ukrainian. In this case, I think gidgi is probably ticked off because he's doing one of baba's chores. Gardening was women's work, while gidgis usually puttered, built things, etc.

POTATO PLANTING 1992
Bronze, h. 10¾ in.
Edition of 20

Skirmish

Back in the Thirties, I understand that the City would donate boxcars for North End kids to use for skating huts. The City would supply the water for the rinks, and the kids would be responsible for getting their own wood to heat these "huts." (It wasn't always a wise idea to ask where this wood came from). A lot of famous hockey players, including Mosienko and Sawchuck, got their start playing on those rinks.

If we had had the boxcar huts in the Forties, I doubt I'd have seen much hockey. I would probably have spent a lot of my time huddled inside, because I had trouble standing up on skates. My skate blades stayed sharp, while the ankles on the boots were worn out. But I always liked to watch the other kids play hockey, and I'd stay out until the cold got to me. They were always trying to emulate their NHL heroes, and, as I watched, I'd try to spot which of their idols they were imitating.

SKIRMISH 1991
Bronze, h. 20 in.
Edition of 20

Paper Boy

Having a paper route didn't work out too well for me. There were too many problems collecting, for one thing. Luckily, my cousin showed me a better way. He sold newspapers from a street corner. Following his lead, I gave up my route and set up shop on a corner, too. It was cold in the winter, but there were no fines, so you got to keep the money you made – and you made more than you would have on a paper route.

This kid reminds me a bit of the old-time town crier. Or maybe he's an early version of today's talking head (for a lot less money, of course).

PAPER BOY 1991
Bronze, h. 14 in.
Edition of 20

Weeding

Babas always fascinated me. They had such a unique sense of clothing style. For example, they'd sport galoshes and grey knit socks in the winter. And their dedication to yard work was amazing. Every time we passed a yard that was full of flowers and immaculately groomed, we'd say there must be Ukrainians living in that house. Babas were always doing some chore or another, and it seemed as if only they could do it right. Baba knows best, I guess.

WEEDING 1992
Bronze, h. 7½ in.
Edition of 20

Fresh Corn

This sculpture shows two women deeply involved in a transaction over corn, at the old Farmers Market. The lady who is so vehemently questioning the price is my sister-in-law's mother. She was called Mrs. Patrick, although I'm not sure how she came by that name, because she was Ukrainian. She lived down the street from us on Magnus.

FRESH CORN 1993
Bronze, h. 20 in.
Edition of 20

Introduction by Luther Pokrant

Drawing is the most fundamental visual art, and one of the most intimate acts of creation. An artist's sketchbook is like a diary, in which he or she records the thoughts, patterns and impressions of life.

The drawings of Armand Paquette are natural and impressionistic, in the sense that they record moments in time and space. I remember encountering some of Paquette's pen and watercolour illustrations in the Parks Canada studio in Winnipeg. The impressions they left me with were of the obvious skill and versatility of the artist; a love of history, roots and identity; good perspective and solid formal construction; and the delicacy of the media.

What particularly impressed me were the techniques and commitment learned over many years of studying such masters as Rembrandt, Van Gogh, Breughel, Kurelek and others, and applying this discipline in a personal and original way to the Manitoba landscape.

Armand Paquette enjoys drawing people and has fond memories of his childhood and the popular culture of the North End. He is clearly a Manitoba artist who relates to his environment through his art, and who lovingly shares these impressions with us.

Luther Pokrant is a well-known artist and illustrator, whose works have been collected by private and corporate sponsors such as the Bronfman family, Cargill Grain and the CIBC.

SHOPPING DAY 1993
Alkyd, 10 x 8
Collection of Loch & Mayberry Fine Art Inc.
Winnipeg, Manitoba

SHOPPING 1993
Pen and Ink, 10 x 8
Collection of Mr. and Mrs. Kozicki
Winnipeg, Manitoba

WEEDING 1993
Alkyd, 8 x 10
Collection of Loch & Mayberry Fine Art Inc.
Winnipeg, Manitoba

CAT AMONG THE CHICKENS 1993
Alkyd, 10 x 8
Collection of Loch & Mayberry Fine Art Inc.
Winnipeg, Manitoba

SCRUB FOOTBALL 1993
Alkyd, 8 x 10
Collection of Loch & Mayberry Fine Art Inc.
Winnipeg, Manitoba

MARBLES 1993
Alkyd, 8 x 10
Collection of Loch & Mayberry Fine Art Inc.
Winnipeg, Manitoba

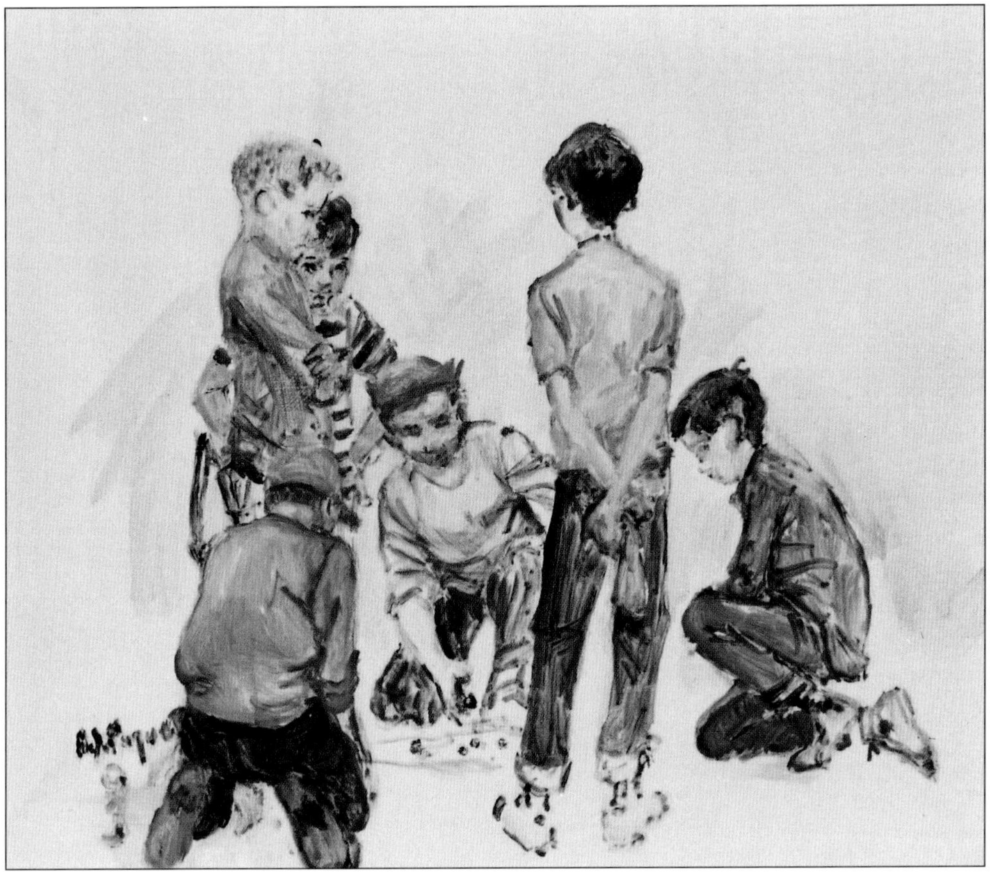

SPRING CLEANING 1994
Alkyd, 10 x 8
Collection of Loch & Mayberry Fine Art Inc.
Winnipeg, Manitoba

FREE ENTERPRISE, MCPHILLIPS 1995
Alkyd, 12 x 16
Collection of Loch & Mayberry Fine Art Inc.
Winnipeg, Manitoba

SNOWBALL WARS 1993
Alkyd, 12 x 12
Collection of John and Bonnie Buhler
Winnipeg, Manitoba

SNOWBALL WARS 1993
Alkyd, 12 x 12
Collection of John and Bonnie Buhler
Winnipeg, Manitoba

POLITICS 1994
Alkyd, 10 x 8
Collection of Loch & Mayberry Fine Art Inc.
Winnipeg, Manitoba

FARMER'S MARKET 1994
Alkyd, 12 x 14
Collection of Loch & Mayberry Fine Art Inc.
Winnipeg, Manitoba

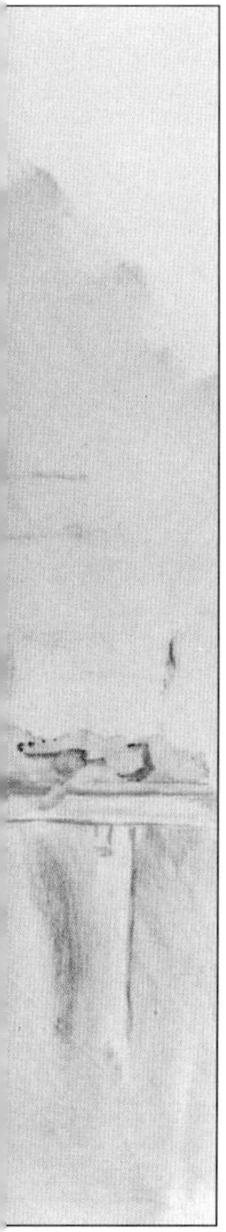

BABA 1994
Alkyd, 10 x 8
Collection of Loch & Mayberry Fine Art Inc.
Winnipeg, Manitoba

SHOPPING 1993
Alkyd, 8 x 10
Collection of Mr. and Mrs. R. Mathieson
Winnipeg, Manitoba

LUXTON SCHOOL 1993
Alkyd, 12 x 16
Collection of Dr. A.M. Brooks
San Mateo, California

ST. JOHN'S COLLEGE 1994
Alkyd, 12 x 16
Collection of Loch & Mayberry Fine Art Inc.
Winnipeg, Manitoba

THE RAG MAN 1993
Alkyd, 12 x 16
Collection of Mr. and Mrs. Peter Liba
Winnipeg, Manitoba

POTATO ROAST 1993
Alkyd, 8 x 10
Collection of Loch & Mayberry Fine Art Inc.
Winnipeg, Manitoba

MARCH STORM OF ' 66 1993
Alkyd, 12 x 16
Collection of Mr. and Mrs. Kozicki
Winnipeg, Manitoba

THE ROYAL ALEX 1992
Alkyd, 12 x 16
Collection of Mr. Justice Nathan Nurgitz
Winnipeg, Manitoba

LATE NIGHT SHOPPING, SELKIRK AVENUE 1993
Alkyd, 12 x 16
Collection of Mr. Justice Nathan Nurgitz
Winnipeg, Manitoba

Gary Styrchak

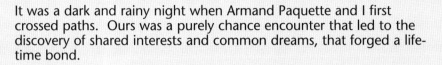

It was a dark and rainy night when Armand Paquette and I first crossed paths. Ours was a purely chance encounter that led to the discovery of shared interests and common dreams, that forged a lifetime bond.

In memory, like a kaleidoscope, I see those rainy evenings turning to cold winter nights. I see those bright sun-drenched Sunday afternoons of spring and rose-coloured skies of autumn, as I stood in front of Eaton's waiting for the bus which would take me to visit Armand and his family. Armand and his wife Vivian, welcomed me into their home, where he and I would spend hours discussing artists, art history and techniques.

I was a dedicated first year Fine Arts student, and, perhaps, apt to take life too seriously. A.J. taught me to "loosen up" my technique by showing me how to look at the life within birds, animals, people and even objects. And, as we worked, I was enchanted by his constant storytelling – about Pinky, Pinhead, the Main Street Market, Armand's misadventures as a paratrooper and tales of his childhood and friends.

When the evenings drew to a close, Armand, Vivian and I would gather around the dining room table, there on Church Avenue, and drink hot, hot tea from clear glass mugs. We'd swap more stories and end up laughing until tears ran down our cheeks.

Since then, I have watched Armand find himself as an artist who is strong in the imagery of our land, its history and peoples – which he cherishes so deeply. And I am honoured to have been involved in the design of this book.

Here, where A.J.'s spirit has marked down scenes and remembrances that carry me back to my youth, and times before, I feel again, with thanks, the winter cold seeping into my bones and I wait, in memory, for the North Main bus to take me and my portfolio to Armand's place in the North End.

Cheers, A.J.

G

Gary Styrchak, a graduate of the University of Manitoba Faculty of Fine Arts, is a Winnipeg-based designer, illustrator and artist.

A.J. Paquette

Vivian's childhood home.